every teen girl's little pink book on girlfriends

by Cathy Bartel

Harrison House
Tulsa, Oklahoma

10 09 08 07 06   10 9 8 7 6 5 4 3 2 1

every teen girl's little pink book on girlfriends
ISBN 13: 978-1-57794-794-3
ISBN 10: 1-57794-794-0
Copyright © 2006 by Cathy Bartel
P.O. Box 691923
Tulsa, Oklahoma 74179

Published by Harrison House, Inc.
P.O. Box 35035
Tulsa, Oklahoma 74153

acknowledgments

Thank You,
Lord,
for wonderful
girlfriends!

contents

introduction

Dear friend,

You are a dear friend, and I am so honored that you would take the time to read what I have written. With every little story and every Scripture I share, I pray that you will be encouraged.

This little pink book is all about girlfriends. Good, old-fashioned, true-blue, loyal, caring, sharing, fun-loving, devoted, kindhearted, sent from-heaven, dearly loved girlfriends! That's the kind I want to be. How about you?

I hope the girlfriends you have can be described in such a way. It takes one to know one! Every good and perfect gift is from above. What a gift our girlfriends are, and we can be that same gift to them!

Love,
Cathy

sisters

Sisters can be absolutely the best friends you have, and friends are definitely like sisters. Don't ever feel left out if you don't have a sister. You really have many sisters. As a Christian, you are a sister in Christ to your other Christian girlfriends. It's called the Sisterhood!

I am very thankful for my little sister. She is six years younger than me. When we were growing up, that seemed to be quite a gap. We didn't have as much in common. We've always loved each other, but now that we're older we have so much fun together. We love to laugh, and we have taught each other different things. She is a great cook. My family loves when Jo Jo comes. She lives in Canada, and I live in Texas, but that has never stopped us from talking on the phone several times a week and will never stop me from thinking of her and praying for her every day.

I also have two wonderful sister-in-laws whom I love and admire so much. They are both awesome wives and mothers, and I really enjoy every moment we spend together.

What a wonderful thing to be able to pick up the phone and share good news with your sisters and girlfriends! It is as precious to me today as it was when I was your age.

God bless all of the wonderful women in our lives!

I received this little story in an email from a good friend and thought it was a good way to start this book.

> A young wife sat on a sofa on a hot, humid day, drinking iced tea and visiting with her mother. As they talked about life, about marriage, about the responsibilities of life and the obligations of adulthood, the mother clinked the ice cubes in her glass thoughtfully and turned a clear, sober glance upon her daughter.
>
> "Don't forget your sisters," she

advised, swirling the tea leaves to the bottom of her glass. "They'll be more important as you get older. No matter how much you love your husband, no matter how much you love the children you may have, you are still going to need sisters. Remember to go places with them now and then; do things with them. And remember that 'sisters' also means your girlfriends, your daughters, and other women relatives too. You'll need other women. Women always do."

What a funny piece of advice! the young woman thought. *Haven't I just gotten married? Haven't I just joined the couple world? I'm now a married woman, for goodness' sake! A grownup. Surely my husband and the family we may start will be all I need to make my life worthwhile!*

But she listened to her mother. She kept contact with her sisters and made more women friends each year. As the years tumbled by, one after another, she gradually came to understand that her mom really knew what she was talking about.

As time and nature work their changes and their mysteries upon a woman, sisters are the mainstays of her life.

After more than 50 years of living in this world, here is what I've learned:

Time passes.
Life happens.
Distance separates.
Children grow up.
Jobs come and go.
Parents die.
Colleagues forget favors.
Careers end.
But...

Girlfriends are there, no matter how much time and how many miles are between you. A girlfriend is never farther away than needing her can reach. When you have to walk that lonesome valley and you have to walk it by yourself, your girlfriends will be on the valley's rim, cheering you on, praying for you, pulling for you, intervening on your behalf, and waiting with open arms at the valley's end. Sometimes they will even break the rules and walk beside you—or come in and carry you out.

Author Unknown

think pink

P — Pray
I — Initiate
N — Note
K — Keep

PROVERBS 27:9 NLT

The heartfelt counsel of
a friend is as sweet as
perfume and incense.

You can kid the world.
But not your sister.

—Charlotte Gray[i]

3 marks of a true friend

There is a big difference between an acquaintance and a true friend. People you simply hang out with will come and go, but a true friend is someone who will always be there for you. Recognizing the difference will help you develop relationships that will last. Here are 3 traits of a true friend.

1. *Honesty.*

A true friend will tell you the truth no matter what, even if it may initially hurt your feelings. Having someone who will give you an honest answer is priceless. (Prov. 27:6.)

2. *Dependability.*

The people who truly value their friendship with you will keep their word. If you cannot count on someone, or if they cannot count on you, your friendship will not last.

3. *Respect.*

Mutual respect is a large part of a good friendship. If someone is not respected, their opinions and feelings will be discounted and overlooked. Without respect, a friendship will simply not work.

will you be my friend?

It is better to have no friends than to have the wrong friends. Remember: When you choose your friends, you are actually choosing your future. Don't settle for anything less than God's best for you. Be patient. He will knit your heart together with those who will help you grow—girlfriends who are like-minded and who want to please the Lord, just as you do. They will help you grow, and you will do the same for them.

I have heard it said this way: *It's good to have friends you can learn from.* It's a wonderful thing to have great godly women whom you can follow. When they have been where you're headed, they challenge you to grow. We can learn so much from others if we humble ourselves and wait on them and listen to them.

We also need to keep ourselves in a place where our younger sisters and girlfriends can learn from us. Make yourself available to the Lord so He can use you to be a leader of other young women. Someone is always watching you.

I remember deciding at one time that I was not the leader type. I didn't want to be a *leader*. That word scared me. Then one day I heard someone say that we are all leaders. There is always someone following us. I found out that just by being a mother I was automatically a leader. I had three little ones watching me all day every day.

You have little sisters, little cousins, and little neighbor girls watching you. Several years after I had grown up, a former neighbor girl told me that my life had influenced her. She was ten years younger than me. I was honored, and more than anything I felt such a sense of responsibility! It made me realize how important it is to be an example, even while you're young. Set an example for others by what you say and do, as well as by your love, faith, and purity!

You are too valuable to sell yourself short by spending precious time with people who don't really care for you. God is faithful and has promised wonderful relationships for you. This little pink book is about girlfriends, but remember that every relationship in your life can be blessed if you only ask the Lord to help you and lead you to choose wonderful friends and to be a true friend to others.

think pink

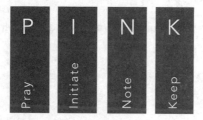

P Pray
I Initiate
N Note
K Keep

Lord, help me to choose wise friends. I want friends who love You. I know I need friends who will help me grow closer to You. I want to be a friend who encourages them, too. Lord, show me how to pray for my friends and to be sensitive to help them. I really want to be supportive in my actions and in my words. Thank You for my friends.

In the cookies of life,
friends are the
chocolate chips.

—Author Unknown

girlfriend

Gift — Your friends are a gift from God, so treat them that way.

Inspire — Inspire each other to do big things.

Rally — Rally around each other. You need to comfort your friends when they are hurting, and be happy for them when they have something to celebrate.

Listen — When your friend talks, listen to what she's saying. This is the easiest and most important part of being a good friend.

Fun — This is the best part of having friends!

Real — Keep it real. Don't be fake. True friends will see right through it.

Include — Expand your group of friends, and get to know others because they can influence your life, too.

Eternal — Make sure you and your friends spend eternity together by sharing the gift of Jesus with them.

Nice — Show kindness and forgiveness to your friends, even if you don't feel like they deserve it sometimes.

Dream — Dream together. Dream about your future and what you want to accomplish in life.

growing good friends

Make it a goal that your girlfriends will be better off after spending time with you, just as you are better off after spending time with the Lord.

Plant good seed in your friendship soil. Help your friends grow. Girls are natural nurturers. God made us to want to help others grow. We love to care for and look after others. Many of us liked caring for our baby dolls. As little girls, we were little mothers from the get-go! That is a good thing—as long as we don't get too bossy with our girlfriends! We need to just help each other and encourage one another as we listen to each other's dreams.

Have short Bible studies with your girlfriends. Pray for each other. Write out Scriptures to encourage them in areas they are struggling with. Be a friend who says:

"You can do it!"

"I'll help you."

"God is faithful."

"You are a blessing."

"Never, never, never give up."

"Let's pray."

Your girlfriends will be forever grateful for you!

I am so thankful for my girlfriends. Oh my goodness! I always hope I tell them enough how each of them has blessed my life! I thank God for every remembrance of these gals in my life! Thank You, Lord!

think pink

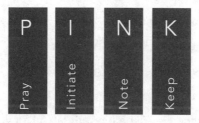

P Pray
I Initiate
N Note
K Keep

If you are having a hard time sharing God's love with someone, ask the Lord to help you see that person through His eyes. Ask Him to give you His heart for her. I guarantee you that when you pray like that, you'll know God's love is working in you and through you. He'll show you the next step. Remember: Hurting people hurt people. Try being kind to the mean girls, and see what happens!

"My best friend is the one who brings out the best in me."

—Henry Ford[ii]

3 messages that lift people up

We grow up in a down world. Comedian Jerry Seinfeld pokes fun at parents who are always using the word "down" with their children: "Get down!" "Settle down." Quiet down." "Turn that thing down!" You get the point. Many of the messages people hear in our world are not very positive. The nightly news is full of stories of war, crime, and tragedy.

When you have a message that encourages, you are sure to stand out from the crowd. Here are 3 messages you can share that will lift a person up.

1. *"God created you to succeed in life."*

But like any created thing, you must find out exactly what you were created to do. A hammer isn't very good at being a screwdriver, but it's powerful when used for its creative purpose.

2. *"No matter what you've done, Jesus Christ loves you without conditions."*

The Bible says that while we were yet sinners, Christ died for us. (Rom. 5:8.) When we were at our worst, Jesus gave us His very best.

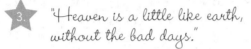
3. *"Heaven is a little like earth, without the bad days."*

The Bible talks about streets, trees, and rivers in heaven. So there are similarities to earth. Yet it promises no pain and no tears! It is absent of tragedy, depression, and temptation. And God has a mansion prepared for every one of His children. (John 14:2; Rev. 21:4,21; Rev. 22:1,2.)

friends forever

There is something so precious about the friends God knits our hearts together with. You watch! You are at an age when some girlfriends may come and go, but you are beginning friendships that are everlasting. They are eternal!

One of my fondest memories is when I was in the seventh grade—or as we said in Canada, grade 7. I had just moved to a new area in our city. I'd had good friends but had never really known what it was to have a best friend.

One day during summer vacation, my friend Laura and I were walking around a park in our neighborhood. We had gotten to know each other that year at school and always had so much fun together. I'm sure that morning I probably scared her a little, but I suddenly had this over-whelming urge to tell her that I considered her my best friend. So I did! She told me I was hers, too, and we were so happy that we hugged and cried a little. I think I skipped all the way home. I was so proud to have a "best friend" and to get to be one.

What is so amazing is that a couple years later we got saved. That made our friendship even more wonderful! When we grew up, we were in each other's weddings. We even both married ministers! Over the years we've lived so far apart, but our friendship is eternal. Sometimes a year or six months goes by before we talk on the phone, but every time we do we laugh and talk like we've never been apart. We can pray for each other, encourage one another, and laugh together, just as if we were back in the seventh grade again. All those miles and all those years will never change what the Lord did in our hearts that day. I love that!

You may have friendships even now that you already know will be forever. Treasure those friendships. We only have a few like that.

Sometimes you have to move away or your friends move away, but remember: Nothing can stop you from communicating these days. You can write letters, e-mail, or talk on the phone. You don't have to lose touch.

It is our responsibility to keep in touch with friends God has given us. We can't get too busy to show our friends we care. When those girl-friends come to mind, pray for them. There is no distance in prayer. There isn't!

Don't be one of those friends who says, "Well, she never calls me." Just be the one to initiate it. You'll be glad you did.

Think about this. Our girlfriends are our sisters in Christ, and we will continue our friendships in heaven forever and ever. That's what I'm talking about: eternal! We can all giggle together in heaven! God's daughters get to hang out together forever. Just think: no curfew! And we won't be cranky the next day after one of those crazy slumber parties! We get to enjoy our friend-ships now and forever!

think pink

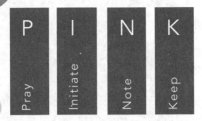

P — Pray
I — Initiate
N — Note
K — Keep

A good way to make sure you are being the best friend you can be is to compare yourself to Galatians 5:22-23. You should strive to have all of these qualities in your relationships with your friends:

Love   Goodness
Joy   Faithfulness
Peace   Gentleness
Patience   Self-control
Kindness

A good tree bears good fruit. None of us have perfected all of these fruits, but our Lord Jesus has, and He will help us in these areas when we ask Him to.

To the world you are just one person, but to one person, you could mean the world.

—Author Unknown[iii]

4 reasons it's critical that you listen to people

Many times, the best preaching and teaching that Christ did was a direct result of His listening to someone. People would come to Him with sometimes simple, and other times very difficult, questions. The Holy Spirit would give Jesus the answer every time. The Bible tells us to "be quick to listen, slow to speak" (James 1:19 NIV). A listening heart attracts many friends and will always be rewarded with wisdom from heaven. Here are 4 reasons to have a listening heart.

1. *Listening gives you time to fully evaluate a person's situation before you pass on counsel or advice that is premature.*

2. *Listening tells the person you care.* It says that person is important and you are not in a rush to send them away.

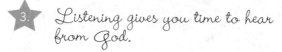

3. *Listening gives you time to hear from God.*

The Lord will speak to you clearly when you take unselfish interest in the lives of others.

4. *God believes in listening.*

What do you think He's doing when we pray? He's listening. Have you ever noticed that He gave us 2 ears and 1 mouth? We ought to listen twice as much as we talk.

unexpected friendships

When I was in high school, there was a lady in my neighborhood whose son had gotten saved. He began to act so different afterwards that she wanted to know what had happened to him. One night she followed him to church and she asked Jesus into her heart. Shortly after, her husband and her two other children did the same thing.

The boy was a good friend of mine, and as his mom started to study the Bible more and more, she had a desire to teach a Bible study to some of the neighborhood girls. I got to be one of those girls and this woman became one of my best friends. I always respected her as an older woman and as a mom, but because she took time to teach me the Word of God, pray with me, and help me in many of my own family crises, I began to admire her as a woman of God and a true friend.

Her and her husband genuinely loved young people and would always welcome us in their home, and I loved being there. I'll never forget when I was about 17 years old she taught us girls about the fruit of the Spirit (love, joy, peace, self-control, kindness, patience, goodness, faithfulness, and gentleness). I loved those Bible studies because I was so hungry to learn God's Word.

Through the next couple of years some of us went away to school, but we always kept in touch with her. She was so interested in our lives and I knew she would pray if I asked her to. Like I said, even though she was older, I considered her a friend because she blessed my life so much.

All these years her oldest son and I had been friends. One year that friendship turned to *really* good friends and, before I knew it, I went from calling her Mrs. Bartel to Mom!

We went from being friends to mother-in-law and daughter-in-law. Today, she introduces me to people as her daughter-in-love. We've never lost that friendship and she truly is one of my best "girlfriends," as well as a great mom and role model. That's a good combination!

I'm thankful she taught me about the fruit of the Spirit and how to pray (not knowing that one day I would be married to her son) which prepared me for quite a ride (it's okay if I say that, Blaine won't be reading this little pink book on girlfriends).

I sure love you, Mom (Miss Elaine). Thank you for being a wonderful mom to all your kids and a girlfriend to us daughters.

my savior, my friend

Our first and very best friend should be the Lord. God didn't have to, but He chose us. When we are born again, we are adopted and God calls us His sons and daughters. He also chooses to call us His friends.

I was thinking about my three boys. Blaine and I will always have a parent-child relationship with them. We will always be Mom and Dad to them, but as they've gotten older we are so proud to call them our best friends—and we pray that our friendship will continue to grow. What a privilege to be God's daughter and what an honor to have a friendship with Him.

Not only are you a daughter of God, but He has called you His friend. Jesus said, "I have called you friends, for everything that I learned from my Father I have made known to you" (John 15:15). Because of your friendship, you can share every secret with Jesus, and He will share secrets with you. As you reveal your true self to Jesus, He will reveal the mysteries of God to you. The Bible says that as you draw near to Him, He will draw near to you. (James 4:8.)

As you pray, read the Bible, and listen to people sharing His Word, you will come to know the Friend who will always be by your side, even in the middle of the night, even in your silliest or loneliest moments. Jesus is closer than a sister or a brother (Prov. 18:24), and He will always be our very best friend.

think pink

P Pray
I Initiate
N Note
K Keep

JOHN 15:13 NIV

Greater love has no one
than this, that he lay down
his life for his friends.

Good friends are like stars. You don't have to always see them, but you know they're always there.

—Author Unknown[iv]

true friend

A friend loves at all times, and a brother is born for adversity.

Proverbs 17:17 NIV

For six years after he graduated from New York's Fashion Institute of Technology, Calvin Klein could get nothing better than bad-paying jobs in New York's garment district. Resorting to working in his dad's grocery story for extra cash, he was far from the dream he'd envisioned for his life.

But a friend believed in young Calvin and gave him $10,000 in startup money to launch his own business. Today you can find Mr. Klein's name on clothing around the world. A true friend will love and help you, even when you are at your lowest point.

girls just want to have fun!

There is nothing like a night out with girlfriends, or maybe just that one special friend. We just have to set aside time for that. No one understands a good heart-to-heart talk or a good laugh like your girlfriends.

I'm not knocking the guys. I have three sons and one husband I love being with. One of the reasons I fell in love with my husband was that I thought he was so funny. We always had fun being together. He still makes me laugh every day. My sons are a lot like their dad. They all have a great sense of humor. I always enjoy getting to hang out with all of them.

As much fun as they are, though, I always make it a point to plan time with my girlfriends. I say *plan* because we really do have to make things happen. I know you know what I'm talking about! If you just say, "Let's get together," and don't come up with a plan, then it won't happen. If those friendships are valuable to us, then we have to make it a priority to keep in touch.

Just a few months back, a dear friend and I were talking about just that. She told me that she and her mom, sisters, aunts, and nieces decided to meet once a month for dinner. It was important to them that, no matter how busy they all were, they spent that time together. Every month a different girl would choose the meeting place. They enjoyed a great time together and caught up on each other's lives.

Right after my friend told me that, the girls in my family started to do the same thing. What a blessing! We've had so much fun. My nieces, Ashley, Brittany, and Savannah, have all had a turn planning the evening. One night we went to look at Christmas lights. Of course, we brought some snacks (definitely some chocolate), and we had so much fun. It's my turn next month, so I'm thinking about ice skating.

It doesn't have to cost anything. Just get together at someone's house to have a little visit. Maybe play some games or watch a movie. It doesn't need to be extravagant. The whole idea is to stay in touch.

The Lord really does knit your heart together with your family's and friends'. He made you to need each other. These are the girls who are going to pray for you when you need them. They are some of your best cheerleaders, your biggest fans. They counsel you and believe in your dreams with you. And all along the way, you're doing the same for them. Enjoy the relationships God has given you.

We need to be so thankful for the women in our lives: moms, sisters, aunties, grandmas, cousins, neighbor girls, friends at school, teachers, coaches, our youth pastors' wives, our pastors' wives, and, as we get older, our mothers-in-law, sisters-in-law, daughters, and daughters-in-law (I want three of those) and even granddaughters (I'll take some of those too!). Our lives wouldn't be the same without them. We need them, and they need us.

I know you can think of lots of ways to spend time together. When you live far apart, don't let that stop you from keeping in touch. We have no excuses these days. We can make a little phone call, send an e-mail, or write a good, old-fashioned letter. Mail is nice, especially when you put some photos in there. I love letters, because when you miss someone you can read them over and over. Remember: Praying for your friends, near or far, always helps to keep them close to your heart.

think pink

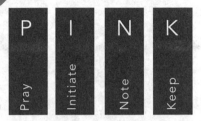

P — Pray
I — Initiate
N — Note
K — Keep

PHILIPPIANS
1 : 3   NIV

I thank my God every time
I remember you.

A friend loves you enough to share her chocolate with you when you're down!

The first Sunday in August is National Friendship Day.

Here are a few ideas to help you celebrate!

★ Send your friends a card, or call them and tell them how much you appreciate their friendship.

★ Invite your friends over for a sleepover, and eat lots of junk food!

★ Put together a photo album containing pictures of you and your friends doing fun things.

★ Make your friend a friendship bracelet, or buy her a necklace with both your initials to symbolize your friendship.

★ Get all dolled up and go out with your friends for dinner and a movie or the theatre.

Go on a picnic and then bike riding, hiking, ice skating, or swimming together.

 Make a CD of your mutually favorite songs.

 Call a radio station and dedicate a song to your friends.

 Write a poem about all the things you like about your friend.

Give your friends a HUG!

a gift from God

Friendship is a gift— an amazing gift—we never want to take for granted. As a young woman, are you finding out that life really is all about our relationships? People are everywhere. They're in your family, at school, at church, at work, at the mall, at restaurants, and in your neighborhood.

When our heavenly Father made us, He intended for us to relate to others. First, we are to love God with all our heart, soul, mind, and strength. Second, we are to love our family, friends, and neighbors as we love ourselves. When we spend time with the Lord (in His Word, worshipping Him, praying, and being taught in a good church), we understand more and more how much He loves us. Having that relationship with God the Father through our Lord Jesus Christ is going to absolutely benefit every other relationship in our lives. When we realize how much God loves us, we can love ourselves and be the kind of friend He wants us to be.

I need to explain something. We are called to love everyone. We can't do that without the love of God in our hearts. I don't want to look down on others. I don't want to be a self-righteous hypocrite. Do you? I didn't think so! Be the girl who rescues others. Be a lifeline, help the mean girls, and don't ever give up on anyone.

The first step is to pray for people. When we find ourselves being critical of people, we need to stop and think, *I wonder if that person has ever had anyone pray for them.* Let's do it. Our heart will be changed, and so will theirs.

think pink

P · I · N · K

Pray · Initiate · Note · Keep

PROVERBS
18:24 NKJV

A [girl] who has friends must
[her]self be friendly.

"A friend is one who walks in when others walk out."

—Walter Winch[v]

Little Pink Book on Girlfriends

3 secrets to making new friends

Everyone wants to be liked. People want friends, and even those who seem a little "stuck up" want to be friendly. So here are 3 secrets that will help you make new friends.

1. Be friendly.

It seems obvious, but many people get so focused on other things that they miss the people and possible relationships passing them by. Grab each opportunity to build new relationships by doing the small things that make it happen. Say "hello," introduce yourself, or simply smile. Make the first effort by showing yourself friendly. (Prov. 18:24.)

2. Focus on others.

People want to talk about things that matter to them. If you spend 4 hours talking about your bad day to someone you just met, don't be surprised if they start avoiding you. Make the effort to find out what they like and focus on things that you have in common.

3. *Do kind things without looking for credit.*

The simple principle of sowing and reaping works in friendships too. If you begin to go out of your way to sow into the lives of people, you will begin to reap the kind of friends that you want. (Gal. 6:7.)

are you a mean girl?

There is absolutely nothing wrong with having a great group of girlfriends! Naturally, you have some friends who are closer to you than others. The question is this: Are you a *mean girl* or a *kind girl*?

Mean girls are just plain mean. They're selfish, gossipy, back-biting, rude, backstabbing, cruel, hateful, and unkind—and that's just within their own little group. They are even more mean to those outside their clique.

Kind girls, on the other hand, are nice. They are helpful, loving, caring, considerate, compassionate, big-hearted, hospitable, generous, understanding, and tenderhearted. The thing that I think is very admirable about kind girls is that they don't hesitate to reach out beyond their circle. We need to always be thinking of ways to reach out to the new girl, the lonely girl, the sad girl, the girl who's made some big mistakes and needs help getting a fresh start. We can reach out to that mean girl, too, who just got kicked out of that group.

These are all potential girlfriends and sisters in Christ! Be a part of that group of girls—or be the girl—at your church, youth group, or school that has hope to offer. There are girls who walk into your church thinking, *This is my last hope to find real love and friendship.* You might be the one to offer that hope.

The Lord wants us to step out of our comfort zone and open our hearts and our circle of friends to others. Our heavenly Father is all about growing, adding, and multiplying. He loved the world (everyone) so much that He gave His one and only Son, that whoever believes in Him will not perish but have eternal life. God's will is that everyone be saved. As His daughters, we want that, too. So let's always be thoughtful of how to show others how good He is. When they find out, they won't want to live another day without Him.

think pink

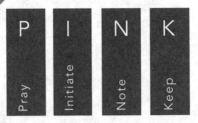

P — Pray
I — Initiate
N — Note
K — Keep

Be a good friend to yourself.
God loves you and wants you to
love yourself. Be kind to yourself,
and be patient as you learn and
grow. You're the one person you
can never get away from. You will
be a better friend to others when
you learn to treat yourself right.

Friendship with oneself is all-important, because without it one cannot be friends with anyone else in the world.

—Eleanor Roosevelt[vi]

3 friendship killers you must avoid

Good friends are hard to come by, and acquiring good friends is only half the battle. The other half is keeping them. If you want to keep your friends, I suggest you don't do these friendship killers.

1. Gossip.

Gossip is simply mischievous talk about the affairs of others. The Bible says that a gossip separates close friends. (Prov. 16:28.) A good friend will keep what he or she knows in confidence, unless someone in authority needs to be notified.

2. Selfishness.

How can we expect to keep the company of others if we are only concerned about ourselves? In Philippians 2:3, Paul wrote that we are to consider others better than ourselves. If we act unselfishly, we will encourage our friendships to grow.

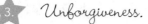

3. *Unforgiveness.*

Our friends will make mistakes. Why? Because they are human. As our friends miss it and then turn from their mistakes or sin, we are to forgive them. We forgive our friends as Christ forgave us. (Eph. 4:31,32.)

no longer lonely

Have you ever been lonely? Maybe you're lonely at this very moment. I want so much for you to not be. God created us as social beings with a need for one another. He doesn't want us to be lonely.

You may be that girl who has cried herself to sleep at night, and as you're reading this book about girlfriends, you're thinking, *Yeah, right. I don't even have one single friend. I don't belong anywhere.*

Can I tell you something? That's not God's will for any of us. He wants for us to know His love through His Son and also through others. Our desire to love and be loved was placed in us by our heavenly Father. He wants us to enjoy our lives, and a major part of that has to do with giving love to the Lord and others, as well as receiving love from the Lord and others.

Don't you ever give up on God's promises for you, and don't you dare put up with one more

second of the god of this world (the devil) steal-
ing, killing, and destroying your dreams for the
wonderful friendships God has for you! The
enemy loves to lie to us and make us feel so
unworthy, rejected, unloved, unaccepted, and
friendless. No more! No way!

Our Bible tells us that we are loved, accepted,
worthy, valued, and cherished. When we recognize where these thoughts are coming from, we
can win this battle. The enemy would love for us
to isolate ourselves from everyone and make us
think we have to be alone, that no one could ever
understand what we're going through, that we
are the only ones in the world facing the circum-
stances we might be in. He wants us to think, *No
one has ever had the problems I have,* or *No one
has ever messed up as bad as I have.* All I can say
to that is, *What a lie!*

I am telling you the truth right now, and the truth
will set you free! We need one another. We need
our family and friends and our church family.
These relationships are so important to all of us. If
you're feeling any loneliness at all, I'd like to take
this opportunity to pray for you.

Lord, I thank You for my dear friend—Your beloved daughter. Thank You for bringing friends into her life. Thank You for knitting her heart together with wonderful, godly women whom she can call her girlfriends. You know what a blessing these girls will be to her and how much they will benefit from her being in their lives.

I command all of these thoughts of inadequacy and words of rejection to be erased from her mind and her heart right now, in Jesus' name. She is clothed in Your love and acceptance. Thank You for reminding her every day that she is adopted by You, Lord. She is the apple of Your eye. She is engraved on the palm of Your hand. Nothing will ever separate her from Your love. You love her with perfect love, and Your perfect love casts out all fear. She will no longer be intimidated. Instead, she will begin to hold her head high and walk in the favor You have bestowed upon her. Thank You, Father, for being our most faithful friend ever and never leaving us alone. Thank You for answering our prayer.

think pink

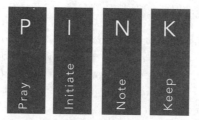

P — Pray
I — Initiate
N — Note
K — Keep

Say these words out loud:

GOD loves me. God LOVES me. God loves ME. I am God's daughter, and I have favor with Him and others. Thank You, Lord, for bringing true, loyal, godly friends into my life. I am a true, loyal, godly friend. God hasn't given me a spirit of fear. Instead, He has given me a spirit of love, power, and a sound mind. I am never alone. Father, You will never, never, never leave me or forsake me.

I love You, Lord, with all of my heart, mind, soul, and strength, and I love my neighbor as myself. Nothing will ever separate me from the love of God—absolutely nothing.

I will not be afraid to reach out to others who are lonely, because Your love is shed abroad in my heart by the Holy Spirit.

Thank You, Lord, for giving me courage to reach out to girls who are lonely. Use me to help heal broken hearts.

I will say what You say about me. The Word is very near me—in my mouth, in my mind, and in my heart—so I can do it. Thank You, Lord!

The glory of friendship is
not the outstretched hand,
nor the kindly smile, nor
the joy of companionship;
it is the spiritual
inspiration that comes to
one when you discover that
someone else believes in you
and is willing to trust you
with a friendship.

—Ralph Waldo Emerson[vii]

if God had a refrigerator

If God had a refrigerator, your picture would be on it.

If He had a wallet, your photo would be in it.

He sends you flowers every spring and a sunrise every morning.

Whenever you want to talk, He'll listen.

He can live anywhere in the universe, and He chose your heart.

What about the Christmas gift He sent you in Bethlehem, not to mention that Friday at Calvary?

Face it, friend. He's crazy about you.

Author Unknown

5 attitudes that are friend magnets

There are always those people you are naturally attracted to, those friends you want to spend all of your free time with. What is it about those people that makes others want to be around them? Here are 5 character traits that make people "friend magnets."

1. Happiness.

Nobody wants to be around a grump. A great attitude is one of the strongest magnets for friends. When you are happy, it's contagious. Always try to stay upbeat, and you will never cease to be in the company of friends.

2. Encouragement.

Choosing to lift other people up with a kind word or a generous action will naturally draw other people to your side. A word in due season is often just the encouragement someone else needs. (Prov. 15:23.)

3. *Generosity.*

Unselfishness is a powerfully attractive force. By choosing to share and to think of others before yourself, you show people that you value them.

4. *Objectiveness.*

It's nice to be around people who are willing to hear the opinions of others. Let's face it: You're not always right, so pick your battles carefully and be willing to accept someone else's idea if it's better than yours.

5. *Helpfulness.*

You're not much of a friend if you're not willing to lend a hand. It works both ways. There will be a time when you need some help, so sow the seeds of friendship now, and you will reap the rewards later.

5 surefire ways to make new friends in a new place

A new place can often be intimidating and lonely. But it can also be a great adventure if you take the initiative to meet new people. Even if you are naturally a shy person, if you follow these simple steps, you will find it easy to make new friends.

1. *Take advantage of every opportunity to introduce yourself to people.*

Introduce yourself to people in the school bookstore, cafeteria, library, and in class. The more people you meet, the greater the odds that you will find people you really connect with.

2. *Remember to use people's names.*

There is no better sound to a person than his or her own name. If you aren't good at remembering names, here is a little trick that will help. When you introduce yourself and your new acquaintance gives you their name, be sure to use it right away.

For example, "Sarah, it sure is good to meet you. Sarah, what classes do you have this semester?" If you can use their name at least three times in your conversation, you will be more likely to remember it. They will also be impressed the next time you see them and use their name.

3. Ask them questions about themselves.

Your conversation will be a hit because you are talking about their favorite subject—them! Everyone's favorite subject is themselves. It is often said, God gave us 2 ears and 1 mouth because He wants us to do twice as much listening as talking. A university study has found that good listening can be worth as much as 20 IQ points. I'll take all the extra points I can get!

4. Have good eye contact. If your eyes are always wandering during your conversation, people will feel you are uninterested in them.

Also, poor eye contact can send them the message that you are insecure or are hiding something from them.

5. Be selective when choosing your closest friends.

Close friends are people who influence your values, self-esteem, and dreams. Be careful to choose friends who love God as you do, believe in your dreams, and build you up. If they are always tearing you down, you can do something about it: Get some new friends. A famous mathematician once said, "You have to have seven positives to overcome one negative." Life is too short to waste it with people who don't believe in you.

what the Bible has to say about friends

As iron sharpens iron, a friend sharpens a friend.

Proverbs 27:17 NLT

Anyone who loves a pure heart and gracious speech is the king's friend.

Proverbs 22:11 NLT

Do not be misled: "Bad company corrupts good character."

1 Corinthians 15:33 NIV

Keep away from angry, short-tempered people, or you will learn to be like them and endanger your soul.

Proverbs 22:24,25 NLT

A friend is always loyal, and a brother [or sister] is born to help in time of need.

Proverbs 17:17 NLT

You can trust a friend who corrects you, but kisses from an enemy are nothing but lies.

Proverbs 27:6 CEV

Whoever walks with the wise will become wise; whoever walks with fools will suffer harm.

Proverbs 13:20 NLT

When two of you get together on anything at all on earth and make a prayer of it, my Father in heaven goes into action.

Matthew 18:19 MSG

A friend loves at all times....

Proverbs 17:17 NIV

Love each other as brothers and sisters and honor others more than you do yourself.

Romans 12:10 CEV

Every good and perfect gift is from above.

James 1:17 NIV

Your task is to single-mindedly serve Christ. Do that and you'll kill two birds with one stone: pleasing the God above you and proving your worth to the people around you.

Romans 14:18 MSG

Make a careful exploration of who you are and the work you have been given, and then sink yourself into that. Don't be impressed with yourself. Don't compare yourself with others. Each of you must take responsibility for doing the creative best you can with your own life.

Galatians 6:4,5 MSG

endnotes

[i] http://www.quotegarden.com/sisters.html

[ii] http://www.friendship.com.au/quotes/quohis.html

[iii] http://www.scrapbook.com/quotes/doc/3770/26.html

[iv] http://www.indianchild.com/friendship_quotations.html

[v] http://www.friendship.com.au/quotes/quofri.htmlell

[vi] http://www.friendship.com.au/quotes/quohis.html

[vii] http://www.coolquotes.com/searchresults.php?pageNum_RSAuthor=2&totalRows_RSAuthor=57&txtkeyword=friendship

prayer of salvation

God loves you—no matter who you are, no matter what your past. God loves you so much that He gave His one and only begotten Son for you. The Bible tells us that "...whoever believes in him shall not perish but have eternal life" (John 3:16 NIV). Jesus laid down His life and rose again so that we could spend eternity with Him in heaven and experience His absolute best on earth. If you would like to receive Jesus into your life, say the following prayer out loud and mean it from your heart.

Heavenly Father, I come to You admitting that I am a sinner. Right now, I choose to turn away from sin, and I ask You to cleanse me of all unrighteousness. I believe that Your Son, Jesus, died on the cross to take away my sins. I also believe that He rose again from the dead so that I might be forgiven of my sins and made righteous through faith in Him. I call upon the name of Jesus Christ to be the Savior and Lord of my life. Jesus, I choose to follow You and ask that You fill me with the power of the Holy Spirit. I declare that right now I am a child of God. I am free from sin and full of the righteousness of God. I am saved in Jesus' name. Amen.

If you prayed this prayer to receive Jesus Christ as your Savior for the first time, please contact us on the Web at **www.harrisonhouse.com** to receive a free book.

Or you may write to us at

Harrison House

P.O. Box 35035

Tulsa, Oklahoma 74153

about the author

For more than a quarter of a century, Cathy Bartel has served alongside her husband, Blaine, in what they believe is the hope of the world, the local church. For the better part of two decades, they have served their pastor, Willie George, in building one of America's most respected churches, Church on the Move, in Tulsa, Oklahoma. Most recently, they helped found Oneighty, which has become one of the most emulated youth ministries in the past 10 years, reaching 2,500–3,000 students weekly under their leadership.

While Blaine is known for his communication and leadership skills, Cathy is known for her heart and hospitality. Blaine is quick to recognize her "behind the scenes" gifting to lift and encourage people as one of the great strengths of their ministry together. Her effervescent spirit and contagious smile open the door for her ministry each day, whether she's in the church or at the grocery store.

Cathy is currently helping Blaine raise a new community of believers committed to relevant ministry and evangelism. Northstar Church will open its doors in the growing north Dallas suburb of Frisco, Texas, in the fall of 2006.

Cathy's greatest reward has come in the raising of her 3 boys—Jeremy, 21, Dillon, 19, and Brock, 17. Today, each son is serving Christ with his unique abilities and is deeply involved in Blaine and Cathy's ongoing ministry.

To contact Cathy Bartel
please write to:

Cathy Bartel
Serving America's Future
P.O. Box 691923
Tulsa, Oklahoma 74169
www.blainebartel.com

*Please include your prayer requests
and comments when you write.*

every teen girl's

little pink book

by cathy bartel

daughters are sugar and spice and everything nice...

well, most of the time!

being mommy or daddy's little *princess* can get challenging sometimes. plug into God's Word and discover what it means to be your heavenly Father's daughter and how special you are to your "fam."

stories, humor, scriptures...everything you need to become the lovely and hip *lady* God has destined you to be.

Available at fine bookstores everywhere or at **www.harrisonhouse.com**.

Harrison House
ISBN: 1-57794-792-4

every teen girl's

little pink book

on gab

by cathy bartel

girls
about to
become

what you think about, you **gab** about, you bring about. you will become what you say.

launch your destiny simply by the things you say. discover how to lay a foundation of success for your future through your words – in love, in school, in relationships, in life. become something great!

Available at fine bookstores everywhere or at **www.harrisonhouse.com**.

Harrison House
ISBN: 1-57794-793-2

every teen girl's

little pink book

on what to wear

by cathy bartel

God ideas for a great wardrobe

find out what's hot:

cool clothes

faith

smiles

beauly inside

modesty

God's love

fashion sense. personal style. get them both.

Available at fine bookstores everywhere or at **www.harrisonhouse.com**.

Harrison House
ISBN: 1-57794-795-9

www.harrisonhouse.com

Fast. Easy. Convenient!

- ◆ New Book Information
- ◆ Look Inside the Book
- ◆ Press Releases
- ◆ Bestsellers
- ◆ Free E-News
- ◆ Author Biographies

- ◆ Upcoming Books
- ◆ Share Your Testimony
- ◆ Online Product Availability
- ◆ Product Specials
- ◆ Order Online

For the latest in book news and author information, please visit us on the Web at www.harrisonhouse.com. Get up-to-date pictures and details on all our powerful and life-changing products. Sign up for our e-mail newsletter, *Friends of the House*, and receive free monthly information on our authors and products including testimonials, author announcements, and more!

Harrison House—
Books That Bring Hope, Books That Bring Change

the harrison house vision

Proclaiming the truth and the power

Of the Gospel of Jesus Christ

With excellence;

Challenging Christians to

Live victoriously,

Grow spiritually.